司马台长城

洪学智

二〇〇〇年三月八日

题词: 洪学智　中国人民解放军上将

Epigraph of Hong Xuezhi, colonel general of PLA of China

出版说明

万里长城是世界上最著名、最宏伟、最壮观的古代奇迹之一。它像一条巨龙，从鸭绿江畔起身，翻越莽莽群山，穿过茫茫草原，跨越浩瀚沙漠，奔向世界屋脊帕米尔高原。万里长城望不断的城楼雉堞、雄关隘口、亭障墩堠，使中国北方显得格外壮丽多姿。

长城的修建，绵延持续了两千多年。长城作为一项军事防御工程，规划之严密，工程之宏伟，修筑之艰巨和延续时间之长，不仅在中国历史上，就是在世界历史上也是少有的。1987年，长城又被联合国教科文组织世界遗产委员会列入"世界历史文化和自然遗产保护项目"，成为全人类共同的财富。

为了帮助海内外人士更全面、更深刻地了解中国万里长城。我们以图文并茂的形式出版中国万里长城系列画册。这些画册既可独立成册，也可成套收藏。保护这些人类无法再造和不能替代的珍贵遗产，是一项崇高的事业。愿这套系列画册的出版能为这一事业奉献绵薄之力。

Publication Introduction

The "Ten-thousand-li Great Wall" is one of the most famous, most magnificent and most grand wonders of ancient times in the world. It winds its way like a huge dragon, running from Yalujiang River, over lofty mountains, across vast grasslands, through boundless deserts, finally reaches Pamirs, ridge of the world. There are countless watchtowers, great gateways, barriers and milestones along the Great Wall. It makes north China more ornate and more beautiful.

The construction of Great has a history of more than two thousand years. As a military defense works, the layout is rigorous, the project is magnificent, the construction is difficult and the period of building is very long. This is seldom seen not only in the history of China, but also in the history of the world. In 1987, the Great Wall was listed as "World historical culture and natural heritage protection project" by World Heritage Committee of UNESCO, and becomes fortune of the entire humankind.

To help people inland and abroad know the Great Wall of China more comprehensively and more deeply, we published this picture album series of Great Wall of China with excellent pictures and accompanying essays. These albums can be bought as singular books or be collected as integrate sets. It is a lofty work to protect these rare heritages which are nonreplaceable and can not be rebuilt by humankind. We hope that publishing this album series will do contribution to the protection work.

序

长城——中华民族伟大力量的象征，它像一条巨龙在神州大地飞起。"起来不愿做奴隶的人们，把我们的血肉筑成我们新的长城"的雄壮歌声，曾经激励过中华儿女而且还将永远激励着中华儿女不断前进，激励着中华民族的伟大复兴。

长城——中华历史的丰碑，上下两千多年。多少历史的波澜，在它身上留下印迹。中华各民族英雄，金戈铁马，逐鹿中原、群雄争立。春秋战国、秦汉隋唐、五代宋辽、金元明清，它始终伴随着中国封建社会兴衰行进。丰碑永存，史传信息。

长城——中华各民族人民智慧与血汗的结晶。它起伏盘旋、飞舞奔腾、纵横十万余里。宇宙航观，峻标屹立，工程宏大，举世无比。中华瑰宝，世界奇迹。

这一中国巨龙、历史丰碑、世界奇迹，古往今来，不知吸引有多少骚人墨客、艺匠画师、元戎将帅、戍卒吏丞、黎民百姓，为之挥毫泼墨、笔走龙蛇，描绘了万里长城的雄风，写出了雄关天险、戍防征战、关山行旅、怀念远人、悲欢离合……等等非常丰富的生活内容的华章。诗词歌赋、记事传奇，千古传诵。近代伟人毛泽东的"天高云淡，望断南飞雁，不到长城非好汉"、"北国风光，千里冰封，万里雪飘，望长城内外，唯余莽莽"更是把长城与壮丽的河山景色相结合，抒发了雄壮的革命胸怀。近代画长城、写长城、唱长城、摄影长城、雕刻长城、织绣长城、印染长城等等的文学艺术作品何止千万。

然而，由于长城的内容实在太丰富了，上下两千多年不断的历史，纵横十万余里的宏伟工程，千百座雄关，千万个烽台，需要向国内外友人、专家学者、参观游人介绍的东西，还非常不够，有些长城地段，关隘城垣的介绍，尚付阙如，或远远不够。司马台长城是万里长城线上十分突出的一个重要地段。我曾经对司马台长城有过："中国长城是世界之最，而司马台长城又堪称中国长城之最"的赞语。当然，其他地段的长城，也各有其独特之处，不能以高下分之。但不管如何，司马台长城的雄险奇特，在万里长城中，确属罕见。

改革开放以来，在邓小平同志"爱我中华，修我长城"题辞的鼓舞下，遵循文物法和古建筑维修的原则，对司马台长城进行了科学的修复并已向国内外游人开放，取得了良好的社会与经济效益，可喜可贺。现有司马台长城管理处，为了满足旅游参观和各方面读者的需要，编辑了一本集长城知识性与艺术性于一体的大型图册。在即将出版之时，书的编者知我多次攀登司马台长城进行考察，对这段长城的保护维修也曾尽了微薄之力，对这段长城有着深厚的感情，特嘱我为序。于是写了一点认识和感想，不当之处，敬请批评指正。至于书中丰富的内容和精美的图片还请读者自己去阅读、观赏和评说。

罗哲文

PREFACE

The Great Wall, a symbol of the great power of the Chinese Nationality, is like a gigantic dragon flying up from the vast land. The majestic national anthem, which sings "Up rise those who are not willing to be slaves, and let's build up a new Great Wall with our flesh and blood", has inspired and will always inspire the Chinese people to forge ahead.

The Great Wall, a landmark of the Chinese history, on it leaves numerous traces of historic ups and downs over the past two thousand years. The ancient heroes of different nationalities, amidst golden spears and armored horses, chased the power and built up their kingdoms. From the Spring and Autumn Period to the Warring States Period, from the Dynasty of Qin, Han to Sui, Tang, Wu, Dai to Song, Liao, Jin, Yuan to Ming, Qing, the Great Wall had been following the advances of the Feudal Society of the Ancient China.

The Great Wall, a crystallization of the wisdom and labour of the Chinese people of all nationalities, winds rising and falling across a distance of 100 thousand li. Ranked as one of the Seven Wonders of the World, this marvelous human-made project could even be viewed from the outer space. Its unparalleled grandness makes it a gem of the Chinese culture.

This Great Dragon of China, a landmark of the history and a matchless wonder of the world has given inspiration to numerous people, including poets, painters, warriors and ordinary people. In their works, they depicted the greatness of the Great Wall, the impregnable passes and natural barriers, the soldiers garrison the frontiers, the travel through the frontier passes and mountains, missing of old friends and all kinds of joys and sorrows. These poetry and verses, articles and legends were widely spread through the ages. Chairman Mao once wrote " Clear sky and light clouds, the wild geese are flying southwards. The man who has not come to the Great Wall can not be regarded as a real hero"."What a magnificent northern scenery with frozen land and falling snow. Looking towards the Great Wall, only see the boundless mountain stretching." His poetry combines the Great Wall with the magnificent scenery of the country and conveys the determination and lofty ideals of the revolutionist. In the modern history of China, a great many literary and art forms were created on the subject of Great Wall, such as painting, writing, singing, photographing, craving and embroidering.

However, as the Great Wall records such a long history of China and there are so many things to tell about the majestic project with thousands of passes and beacon towers, the introduction of some parts of it and certain passes to friends from both at home and abroad, experts and scholars, visitors and viewers is far from enough. SiMatai is a very important part on the Great Wall scenery line,I once praised it as " The Great Wall of China is the wonder of the world and SiMatai is the wonder of the Great Wall".It is true that other parts of the Great Wall are also unique for their respective features and can not be compared for superiority, but still SiMatai is outstanding for its precipitous and difficult access.

Since the reform and opening-up, encouraged by the words of our leader DengXiaoping" Love our motherland and build our Great Wall" and adhering to the Law of Historic Relics and the Principle of Ancient Building Renovation, SiMatai has been scientifically repaired and open to the public. Good social and economic results have been achieved.In order to meet the demands of travellers and visitors, the Administration Office of SiMatai now edits a large album focusing on the knowledge and art of the Great Wall. On the occasion of the publication, the editor of the book, who happens to know my constant visit and study on husiasm about it, asks me to write a foreword to this book. And herewith I write about some of my feelings and knowledge about it. Anything improper about my words, it is open to criticism and correction. As for the rich content and beautiful pictures of the book, it is up to the readers to read, appreciate and make their judgement.

Luo Zhewen

望京楼与聚仙楼
The Watching Beijing Tower and The Juxian Tower

眺望司马台长城
Overlook the Simatai Great Wall

俯瞰晨光中的司马台长城
Survey the Great Wall in the morning sunshine

司马台长城景区游览示意图
Simatai Great Wall Tourist Map of the Scenic Stop

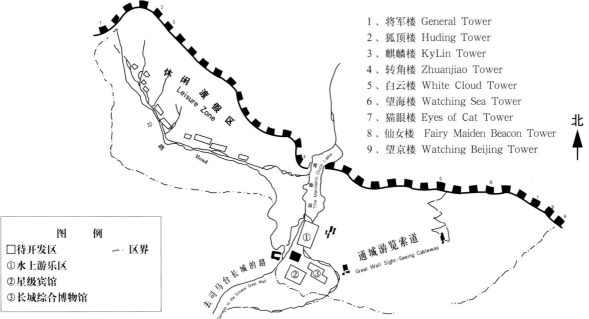

1、将军楼 General Tower
2、狐顶楼 Huding Tower
3、麒麟楼 KyLin Tower
4、转角楼 Zhuanjiao Tower
5、白云楼 White Cloud Tower
6、望海楼 Watching Sea Tower
7、猫眼楼 Eyes of Cat Tower
8、仙女楼 Fairy Maiden Beacon Tower
9、望京楼 Watching Beijing Tower

北

图　例
□待开发区　　　　　— 区界
①水上游乐区
②星级宾馆
③长城综合博物馆

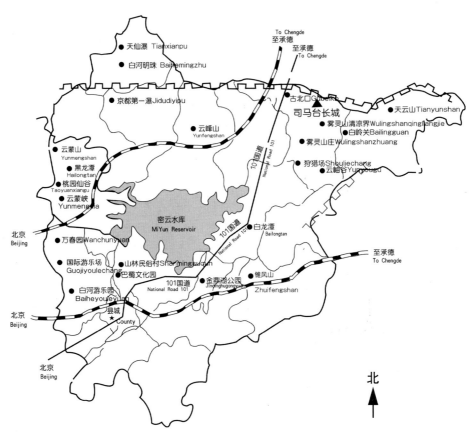

司马台长城旅游景区地理位置图
Simatai Great Wall geographical Position of the Tourist Scenic Spot

10

望京楼是司马台长城最高的敌楼，据说晴晚西望，可见北京城的灯火，故称望京楼

Watching Beijing Tower   It is located on a vantage point. In a clear night one can see the lights in Beijing from the tower.

司马台长城

SIMATAI GREAT WALL

司马台长城位于北京东北部120公里的险关重镇古北口境内，此段长城始建于明洪武初年，是一段偏离原北齐长城基础的明长城，也是至今仍保留明代长城原貌的一段古长城。

司马台长城，全长5.4公里，敌楼35座。整段长城构思精巧、设计奇特、结构新颖、形态各异，它集万里长城众多特色于一地，形成一段"奇妙的长城"。

综观司马台长城，可用"险、密、全、巧、奇"五字概括。**险**：司马台长城沿刀削斧劈似

1942年冀东八路军途经司马台长城险关
The Eighth Route Army of east Hebei by way of strategic pass of Simatai Great Wall in 1942

Simatai Great Wall is located in Gubeikou, a strategic pass about 120 km to the northeast of Beijing. The construction of this part of Great Wall started in the early Hongwu Reign of Ming Dynasty. It is a section of the Great Wall of Ming Dynasty that was not built on the foundation of Great Wall of North Qi. It is a section that still keeps the original appearance of Great Wall of Ming Dynasty.

Simatai Great Wall is 5.4 km long. There are 35 watchtowers on it all together. This section of Great Wall was ingeniously conceived and uniquely designed with novel structure and diversification. It concentrates many characteristics of the Great Wall in one section, and forms a section of "Wonderful Great Wall".

Simatai Great Wall can be described with the following five words: precipitous, dense, compehensive, ingenious and peculiar.

Precipitous: Simatai Great Wall was built along the wriggling mountain ridge that seemed to be cut by knives and axes. It wind its way sinuously and dangerously. It is particularly dangerous in the sections of Sky Ladder and Sky Bridge. Sky Ladder is single side Great Wall.

坡陡墙窄
The steep mountainside and narrow wall

挺立在陡峭山岩上的仙女楼
The Fairy Maiden Beacon Tower standing on precipitous rock

The ramp is steep and the wall is narrow. The narrowest part is no more than half a meter in width. It goes up along the mountain like straight ladders. There are sheer precipices on both sides of it. When looks down from it, anyone will feel dizzy. Above the Sky Ladder is the Sky Bridge, which is less than 100 m long and just has the width of a brick, about 40 cm. There are also sheer precipices on both sides, which will make you tremble with fear and lose the spirit of hero. Tourists named the Sky Bridge as "been so close and yet so far away". It is often described by those who have been here in the following way—"Passing through the bridge is more difficult than reaching the sky". This section could be recognized as one of the most precipitous part of the Ming Dynasty Great Wall, which was built based on the natural dangerous landform and made the mountain more precipitous.

Dense: It is another unique character of Simatai Great Wall. The smallest distance between two watchtowers is only 43.8 m, the

敌楼密集的司马台西长城
West Simatai Great Wall with dense watchtowers

的山脊修筑，蜿蜒曲折，惊险无比，尤其是天梯和天桥两段，更是险中有险。天梯是单面墙长城，坡陡墙窄，最窄处不足半米，呈直梯状沿山体上升，两侧更是陡峭悬崖，置身其上，俯首下望，令人目眩。天梯顶端，便是天桥，长不逾百米，宽只有一砖，约40厘米左右，两侧又是悬崖绝壁，令人不寒而栗，英雄气短，游客把这儿称作咫尺天涯。虽然名为天桥，但到这里的人们却都说："过桥难，难于上青天"，这里可说是明长城中依山设险，险上加险的最险要地段之一。**密**：是司马台长城又一特点，两敌楼相距最近仅43.8米，最远600米，一般都在100—200米之间，若按当时明代筑长城的

most distant two towers are just about 600 m apart from each other. The average distance between towers is about 100–200 m. According to the regulations of building Great Wall of the

规定，每500米修敌楼一座的话，可见此段长城是一例外。**全**: 是指敌楼和城墙的建筑形式

箭窗数目不一的敌楼
Two-balistraria tower and three-balistraria tower

四眼楼
Four-balistraria tower

五眼楼
Five-balistraria tower

Ming Dynasty, one watchtower was to be built at about every 500 m. Therefore, this section of Great Wall was an exception.

Comprehensive: This means that the construction forms of both the towers and the wall are unique and diversified. For their outside appearances, some towers have one observing hole, some have two, three, four or five holes. Some watchtowers have only one story, some have two and some have three stories. They all have rooms inside. These towers are varying in size and form. They were built according to ranks of the head officers and numbers of soldiers as well as the strategic conditions of locations. From the view of interior structure, some were built with bricks, some with bricks and wood, some with bricks and stones; Some has a single room, some has two or multiple rooms. The internal room layout of some towers are like Chinese character "田(field)", and some like "井(well)". The roofs of watchtowers are also varying in forms. Some are flat, some are arched, some are octagon caisson roofs and some have double cup like roofs. Even the entrances and windows are novel and unique. Some were built on the side and some in the middle. Some were built with bricks, some with stones, some were even built with exquisite carved granite. These are all rare and precious historical relics in history of the Great Wall. The Fairy Maiden Watchtower and the Overlooking Beijing Tower, located at eastern part of the Wall, are two typical watchtowers. Overlooking Beijing Tower is the highest place of the Simatai Great Wall. It is 986 m above the sea level. It is a three-hole, two-story, brick-stone tower. It gained the name because it gives you a wide view and you can roughly see the profile of Beijing. Standing on top of the tower and looking eastward, you

在麒麟楼上有一雕刻着麒麟的影壁，这是万里长城罕见的遗迹
Screen wall carved with KyLin on KyLin Tower. It is a peculiar vestige of the Ten-thousand-li Great Wall

奇特多样。从外观来看，敌楼有单眼楼、双眼楼、三眼楼、四眼楼和五眼楼，有单层楼，上下相通的双层楼和三层楼。它们均为空心敌楼，大小不一、形态组合各异，是按驻军的官衔等级，驻防人数以及地势险要程度分别来建造的。从内部结构来看，有砖结构、砖木结构、砖石结构；又有单室、双室、多室之分；房间布局有"田"字、"井"字；楼顶变化多端，有平顶、穹窿顶、八角藻井顶、覆斗顶；就连门窗也新颖别致，有边门、中间门、有砖券和石券，还有技艺精湛的雕花花岗岩石门。这是长城史上不可多得的珍贵文物。司马台长城东段的仙女

will see the "Mist and Snow", "Coiling Dragon and Sleeping Tiger"; looking northward, you will see "Endless Green of Yanshan Mountain"; looking southward, you will see "Pearl of the Reservoir". The beautiful scenery will come into your eyes completely. The Fairy Maiden Tower is the most beautiful one among the watchtowers. It set off the boskages at side of the Tiger Mountain. The lower part of it was built with long pieces of stones and the upper part

望京楼与仙女楼
The Watching Beijing Tower and The Fairy Maiden Beacon Tower

覆斗顶
Double cup like roofs

楼和望京楼就是两种具有代表性的敌楼，望京楼是司马台长城上的制高点，海拔986米，为空心三眼楼，二层砖石结构。这里视野开阔，隐约可见北京城轮廓，故称望京楼。望京楼头，东观"雾灵积雪"、"蟠龙卧虎"、北看"燕山叠翠"、南瞰"水库明珠"、壮丽关山、尽收眼底。仙女楼是敌楼中建造得最精美的一座，掩映在老虎山腰的树丛中，下部条石合缝，上部磨砖达顶。内部用青砖砌成两道大拱，三条甬道，十个券门。顶部正中心砌成蛛网状的八角藻井，四边砌四个砖柱，游人在里面轻轻放歌便能发出悦耳的回音。门券上还有并蒂莲花浮雕，整个敌楼处处给人以精巧、细腻、秀丽之感。仿佛它不是人间战争的防御设施，而是一座仙境楼阁。此外，城墙的构造更是匠心独运，富于变化。因地形和军事上的需要，城墙又分为单边墙、双边墙和障墙，有砖砌、石砌及砖石混合砌，城墙上的箭孔疏密也从几十个直到上百个。巧:

障墙
The barrier wall

体现为进可攻，退可守，步步为营的障墙。而小天梯上的障墙，可谓登峰造极，在20多米的垂直落差内从最顶上的障墙箭孔，一直可以通

with polished bricks. Inside it, there are two arched roofs, three paved paths, ten arched doors, which were built with cyan bricks. The roof was built into a spider-web-like octagon caisson ceiling. On its four sides there are four brick pillars. If you sing lightly inside, there will be pleasant echoes. Above the doors there are sculpture of twin lotus flowers. The whole tower gives you the impression of exquisiteness, fine, smooth and beautiful. It looks more like a building in paradise than a defense work for war. In addition, construction of the wall is also unique and diversified. Due to their locations and the military requirements, different parts were built in forms of singular, double or barrier wall with bricks, stones or a mixture of them. The density of balistrarias also varied from dozens to ahundred.

Ingenious: This is embodied in the construction of the barrier wall that could be used for both offense and defense, consolidating step by step. Construction of the barrier wall above the Sky Ladder had reached the peak of perfection. With the 20 m drop in elevation, one can shoot arrow from balistraria in the top barrier wall. Through all balistrarias in barrier walls, the arrow can reach the balistraria at the bottom. The ingenuity is really marvelous. From this you could imagine the scenes of ancient soldiers fighting violently against enemy.

Peculiar: The Great Wall built above water-eroded caves. The ingenious combination of water-eroded caves and the wall is unique among the entire Great Wall of Ming Dynasty. We can't help thinking that it is splendid.

Although the major scenery of Simatai is Great Wall with precipitous mountain, there are also beautiful scenes with waves of clean water and sailing boats. The Mandarin Duck Lake at the foot of this section brings spirit to the Great

过所有障墙的射孔，到达最下的射孔，精巧之至，另人赞叹。由此可以想像昔日戍边将士苦战御敌的战争场面。**奇**：构筑在溶洞上的长城，

天桥，又称通天洞
Sky Bridge, also called Sky Cave

洞与城的巧妙组合,在整个明长城中绝无仅有,令人称奇叫绝。

司马台长城虽以山势险陡、长城雄奇为主景,却不乏碧波荡漾、湖光帆影的优美环境,长城角下的鸳鸯湖赋予了这段长城以灵性,清澈的湖水,是由水量充沛、四季凉爽的冷泉和冬季热气喷涌、水温常年在38℃的温泉汇聚而成的,湖水冷暖各半,经冬历夏,从不结冰。夏季里,荡舟湖上,清风徐来,让人神清气爽,心旷神怡。

司马台长城不仅有奇丽的风光,亦是一座文化遗产的宝库。近年来,在这段长城上发现了

Wall. The clean water comes from the abundant perennial cool spring and hot spring, which sprays hot vapor in winter and keeps water temperature at 38℃ year round. Water of the lake is cool in one half and hot in another half. It never freezes whether in summer or winter. Sailing on the lake in summer, the cool breeze will make you relax and happy.

Simatai Great Wall is not only a unique and beautiful scenery, but also a treasury of cultural heritage. In recent years, many cultural relics about Great Wall are found in this section, including Carved stone "superscription tablet", which recorded the situation of building Great Wall in those years and names of officials correlated to construction. In several parts of the walls and towers, bricks with stamped words

长城脚下的鸳鸯湖
The Mandarin Duck Lake

司马台长城保存的各式铁炮
All kinds of cone drums stored on the Simatai Great Wall

许多长城文物，其中：有石刻"题名碑"，碑上记载着当年修建长城时的情况以及与建城有关的官员的名字，同时这里还发现几处城墙和敌楼上有带戳印文字的砖，上面刻的都是参加修建长城的军队名称和年代，如"万历五年山东左营造"、"万历五年宁夏营造"等等。长城砖上带有戳印文字，在其它长城上也是及为少见。

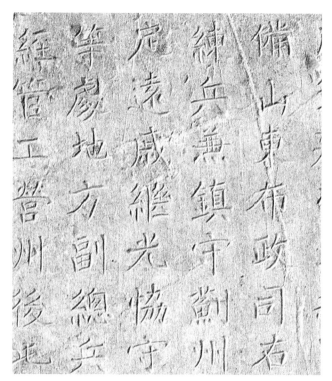

司马台长城保存筑城时的石碑，碑文中有明朝著名将领戚继光的名字
Stone tablet saved during the construction of Simatai Great Wall. In these inscriptions, there is name of the famous general, Qi Jiguang, of the Ming Dynasty.

刻有文字的城砖已被风蚀雨浸
Great Wall bricks with stamped words has been eroded by wind and marinated by rain

在修复这段长城清基过程中，又清出一批出土文物：有当年守城将士使用过的各种武器，其中有铁炮、石炮、铁镞、铁铳、手雷、三眼铳。铁弹丸、火药勺等，还有守城战士用过的生产

on bricks are seldom seen in other sections of the Great Wall. During the course of stripping in repairing this section of Great Wall, many cultural relics were unearthed: there are all kinds of weapons used by soldiers who had defended the Great Wall, including cone drums, stone slingers, iron arrowheads, grenades, three-barrel blunderbusses, iron cannonballs, gun-power spoons, etc. There are tools for producing and living used by the soldiers, including hoes, shovels, kitchen knives, iron lamp-cups, etc. The cultural relics mentioned above are very precious. They provide valuable practicality for studying Great Wall and history of Ming Dynasty.

司马台长城保存的石雷
Stone mine stored on the Simatai Great Wall

The Great Wall is very important culture heritage not only in China, but also in the world. Simatai Great Wall is a bright pearl in this heritage. To protect this section of Great

生活用具，其中有锄头、铁铲、菜刀、铁灯碗等等，以上这些文物很珍贵，它为研究明代长城及明代历史提供了价值很高的实物资料。

长城是中国也是世界上非常重要的文化遗产，司马台长城则是这份遗产中的一颗明珠，为了更好地保护这段长城，并满足广大中外游客更好地领略长城的风采，司马台长城景区一手抓文物保护工作，一手抓旅游开发建设，使司马台长城这一世界文化瑰宝无愧于时代，无愧于著名长城专家罗哲文教授的评价："中国长城是世界之最，而司马台长城是中国长城之最。"

（部分资料图片由司马台长城管理处提供）

被日寇击残的司马台白云楼，是日本法西斯侵略中国的历史见证
The White cloud tower of Simatai, which was destroyed by Japanese invaders, is a historical testimony proved that Japanese fascist have ever invaded China.

英国飞车王子埃迪·基狄驾车飞越司马台长城
Flying car prince of Britain, Eddy Kiddy is driving a car to rush over the Simatai Great Wall.

Wall and satisfy tourists' requirements inland and abroad to appreciate graceful profile of the Great Wall, the scenic spot of Simatai Great Wall strengthens the protection work and develops tour simultaneously. This made the Simatai Great Wall feel no regret to the age and to evaluation of famous experts of the Great Wall, professor Luo Zhewen: "The Great Wall of China is wonder of the world, and Simatai is wonder of the Great Wall of China".

万人攀登长城
Ten thousand people climbing the Great Wall

春 · 垛口下盛开的桃花
Spring · Blooming peachblossoms below crenels

夏 · 绿树丛中的天梯与障墙

Summer · Barrier Wall in green boskages

秋·色彩斑斓的荒城
Autumn · Colorful waste town

冬 · 高耸入云的天梯
winter · The Heavenlly Ladder

从卧虎岭远眺司马台长城
Overlook the Great Wall from Pronating Tiger Mountain

闪电映照下的天梯

Sky Ladder in the brilliance of lightning

单边墙与仙女楼

Single side wall and The Fairy Maiden Beacon Tower

黎明时的司马台西长城
West Simatai Great Wall before sunrise

黎明时的聚仙楼
The Juxian Tower before sunrise

危立在悬崖上的望京楼

Watching Beijing Tower ruggedly standing on the precipice

初秋时敌楼内景

Internal scene of watchtower in the first month of autumn

蜿蜒在荒山上的司马台长城

Wandering Simatai Great Wall in barren mountains

形态各异的敌楼
Watchtowers with a great variety of forms

有上、中、下三排射孔的单边墙
Single side wall with three rows of balistrarias above, medially and below

长城上雪后楼梯的韵律美
The aesthetic feeling of cadence when stairs of the Great Wall are covered with snow

图中敌楼设计巧妙，敌楼无门与城墙直接相通。欲进此楼，必须由城墙内侧的拱门而出，沿小径至楼下，然后再登攀临时设置的小梯，方可爬入敌楼内，这样，大大增强了敌楼的防御功能

This cleverly designed watch tower has no doors on either side to the top of the Geat wall. It can be entered only through a tunnel in the wall along a tiny path and a narrow ladder. The entrance is no wider than a hole for archers.

司马台东长城密集的敌楼

Dense watchtowers in East Simatai Great Wall

夕阳下的箭垛

Crenels in shining of the setting sun

狐顶楼内景
Internal scene of Huding Tower

站在狐顶楼顶向东远眺
Overlooking eastward when standing on top of Huding Tower

山雨欲来风满楼
The wind sweeping through the tower heralds a rising storm in the mountain

李少白 摄影

司马台东长城在日出时分的壮丽景象
The imposing scenery of East Simatai Great Wall at the moment of sunrise

望京楼之晨
The morning of the Watching Beijing Tower

古城春意
Spring in air of the old town

夕阳染红了雪后的司马台西长城
Light of the setting sun incarnadined the snow-covered West Simatai Great Wall

远望筑有障墙的长城，好像龙脊一般

Overlooking the Great Wall with barrier walls, which looks like ridge of dragon

初阳下的雪城与阴影中
的古砖相映成趣

*The snow-covered
town under the rising
sun and ancient bricks
in shallows are shining
upon each other*

夕阳染红了雪后的司马台东长城

Light of the setting sun incarnadined the snow-covered East Simatai Great Wall

高筑在陡峭山脊上的司马台东长城
East Simatai Great Wall built on the high steep ridge of mountain

聚仙楼夏景
Summer of The Juxian Tower

司马台西长城暮色
Gloaming of West Simatai Great Wall

春
_____
Spring

李少白 摄影

侧望天梯
Watching the Sky Ladder from its side

天光云影下的司马台西长城
West Simatai Great Wall in the daylight and cloud shadow

美人守夜
A beauty standing night vigil

迎着朝阳一字排开的司马台西长城
West Simatai Great Wall collocated in a line towards the rising sun

李少白 摄影

从望京楼上东眺聚仙楼
Watching the Juxian Tower from Overlooking Beijing Tower

山舞银蛇
The snow-covered mountain are winding like snake

险窄的单边墙与望京楼
The steep and narrow wall and the Watching Beijing Tower

雾袭聚仙楼
The Juxian Tower in fog

历尽沧桑的古城墙
The vicissitudinous ancient city wall

银装素裹的长城脚下，鸳鸯湖依然碧波荡漾，雾气蒸腾

Although the foot of Great Wall is covered with snow, there are still poppling blue waves and rising vapor in the Mandarin Duck Lake

通天洞和它上面的雪城
Tongtian Cave and the snow-covered town above it

雪后司马台西长城
Snow-covered West Simatai Great Wall

司马台东长城全景

Panorama of East Simatai Great Wall

望京楼与晚霞
The Watching Beijing Tower and　the evening glow

李少白 摄影

楼外楼
Tower outside tower

司马台西长城月夜
West Simatai Great Wall under moonlight

俯瞰司马台长城
Survey the Simatai Great Wall

蜿蜒而上的司马台西长城
Wandering upward West Simatai Great Wall

晨光中的望京楼与聚仙楼
Watching Beijing Tower in the light of morning sun

残破的敌楼在夕阳中充满了古意诗情
Beat up watchtowers in the light of setting sun, full of interest, charm and poetics of antique taste.

司马台长城夏晨
Morning of Great Wall in summer

敌楼内巧夺天工的八角藻井顶

Octagonal caisson roof inside the watchtower, wonderful work excelling nature

巍峨的司马台东长城，耸立在最高处的敌楼即望京楼

Majestic East Simatai Great Wall, the watchtower standing highest is Watching Beijing Tower

雄伟的司马台东长城
The grand East Great Wall

李少白 攝影

仙女楼位于望京楼西，是司马台长城敌楼中最美的一座。传说一只美丽的羚羊变成仙女住在此楼，与牧羊人相恋，所以称仙女楼

Fairy Maid Tower Located to the west of Watching the Capital Tower, it is the most graceful watch tower on the Great Wall. A folk tale asys

and antelope and a fairy maid once lived in it. The fairy and fell in love with a local shepherd

78

李少白与儿子在一起
Li Shaobai with his son together

独特的审美视角

——李少白的长城摄影

　　长城不仅是举世公认的人类伟大遗迹，而且也是世界上为数不多的、令人神往的、且具有经久不衰魅力的、备受艺术家青睐的创作主题。不知有多少中外摄影爱好者和摄影家来到了长城，将镜头对准了雄关要塞、烽火墩台、城墙敌楼……，摄下了数不胜数的长城图片，并且涌现出众多优秀的长城摄影家。李少白先生就是他们中间特别出色的一位。他爱长城至深，摄长城至诚。他数百次登上长城，东起鸭绿江边，西至嘉峪关外，足迹遍及长城的重要关隘。摄下了大量的长城图片，创作出许多不同凡响的长城摄影作品。李少白先生不仅是一位极具个性，富有才华的摄影家，而且是一位一直坚持自己见解，勇于探索的艺术家。相对其他摄影家而言，他的镜头对美和对美的表达更感兴趣。当李少白先生拍摄长城时，不是把长城作为用于宣传册或教科书的例证，而是作为人类伟力和大自然的神奇结合的象征。

　　作为一个艺术家，李少白先生一次次用相机镜头对准长城时，经常敏锐地捕捉到历史与现实复合在一起的神秘意境，且从风云雪雾的变幻中，岁月流逝的浸淫下领悟到古老长城的无限美感，进而找到了表现这些的独特的审美视角和艺术语言。李少白先生所摄下的长城：或雄伟、或奇绝、或苍凉、或古朴、或沉雄、或幽深，变化无穷，叹为观止。最大程度地从各种角度展现了长城的壮丽景致和深厚的历史沉积。

　　长城是祖先用血汗白骨，为我们留下的伟大奇迹。李少白先生的长城摄影作品，则是，凭着他对长城的热爱，凭着他执着的艺术追求，将单纯的自然中的长城，化成了富有精神内涵的，展现长城无尽神韵的艺术结晶。

— ·家正·—
2000年于北京

THE UNIQUE AESTHETIC ANGLE OF VIEW
——The Great Wall in the picture taken by Li Shaobai

　　The Great Wall is not only world-recognized grand heritage of mankind, but also one of the rare creation motifs as the favor of artists. Peoples are attracted by it and its fascination never breaks down. Uncountable numbers of shutterbugs and camerists come to the Great Wall and focus their cameras to great gateways, beacon towers, walls and watchtowers, etc. They made countless photographs of the Great Wall. Thus, many excellent Great Wall camerists appeared. Mr. Li Shaobai is an outstanding one among them. He loves the Great Wall deeply and shoots it with sincere desire. He had come to the Great Wall hundreds of times. From the bank of Yalujiang River in the east to Jiayuguan Gateway in the west, his footprints are all over the important gateways of the Great Wall. He made large quantity of pictures and created many outstanding photograph creations of the Great Wall. Mr. Li Shaobai is a distinctive and ingenious camerist. He always insists on his own conceptions and is brave in exploration. Compared with other camerists, he is more interested in beauty and its expression. When he shoots the Great Wall, he doesn't regard it as examples in propagandistic books or textbooks, but as the symbol of magic combination of human power and great nature.

　　As an artist, Mr. Li Shaobai can often capture the mysterious conception combining the past and reality when he shoots the Great Wall. From the varying of wind, cloud, snow and fog, from the lapse of month and year, he realized the infinite aesthetic feeling of the age-old Great Wall. Then he found the unique aesthetic angle of view and artistic language to represent them. The Great Wall in the pictures shot by Mr. Li Shaobai is sometimes grand, sometimes wonderful, sometimes desolate, sometimes simple and unsophisticated, sometimes oppressive, sometimes deep and serene. It varies infinitely and can be acclaim as the peak of perfection. This expresses the imposing scenes and deep historical accumulationed of the Great Wall in the deepest degree.

　　The Great Wall is the grand wonder built by our ancestors with sweat, blood and bone. Depending on his love to the Great Wall and inflexible seeking in art, Mr. Li Shaobai shot pictures which are artistic crystallization full of spiritual meanings and expressing the infinite verve of Great Wall from its simple and natural form.

Jiazheng
Beijing, 2000.

图书在版编目(CIP)数据

司马台长城：汉英对照／李少白摄．—北京：中国摄影出版社，2000.3
ISBN 7-80007-369-6

Ⅰ.司…　Ⅱ.李…　Ⅲ.长城，司马台－摄影集　Ⅳ.K928.71-64

中国版本图书馆 CIP 数据核字(2000)第 05051 号

中国长城之最—— **司马台长城**

The best of the Great Wall —Simatai

作　　者：李少白
责任编辑：卢志仁
翻　　译：王晓虹
封面设计：杨侵海
版式设计：余贵芳　殷明霞
出　　版：中国摄影出版社（东单红星胡同 61 号）
承　　制：北京紫禁城文化发展有限公司
制版印刷：北京永明纸品有限公司
发　　行：全国各大新华书店
开　　本：大 16 开
印　　张：5 印张
版　　次：2000 年 3 月第一版
印　　数：10000 册
书　　号：ISBN 7-80007-369-6／J·369
定　　价：118 元

Photos by:Li Shaobai
Editor in Charge:Lu Zhiren
Translated by:Wang Xiaohong
Cover design by:Yang Qinghai
Besign by:Yu Guifang　Yin Mingxia
Published by:China Photographic publishing house